BE PRODUCTIVE, NOT JUST BUSY: AN EFFECTIVE GUIDE TO HIGH OUTPUT MANAGEMENT

CLINT J. WILSON

INTRODUCTION

LEARNING THE BASICS OF HIGH OUTPUT MANAGEMENT

In today's fast-paced and technology-driven business landscape, organizations are constantly seeking ways to optimize their operations and maximize productivity. One crucial aspect of achieving efficiency and effectiveness is through the implementation of high output management practices. Learning the basics of high output management is essential for businesses to streamline their processes, reduce costs, enhance productivity, and deliver superior results.

High output management refers to the strategic approach of controlling and optimizing the generation, distribution, and storage of documents and other forms of output within an organization. It encompasses a range of activities, including printing and formatting control, document routing and distribution, print job tracking and auditing, security and access control, electronic document delivery, and archiving and storage. By mastering these fundamental principles, businesses can transform their output processes, gain a competitive edge, and achieve operational excellence.

Understanding the basics of high output management enables organizations to streamline their document-related workflows, ensuring that the right information reaches the right people or systems in the most efficient and effective manner. By implementing an efficient output management system, businesses can reduce manual intervention, automate tasks, and optimize resource utilization. This results in improved operational efficiency and increased productivity as employees can focus on higher-value tasks rather than being burdened by time-consuming document-related activities.

Moreover, learning the basics of high output management allows businesses to minimize costs associated with printing and document distribution. By consolidating print jobs, optimizing printing resources, and reducing waste, organizations can achieve significant cost savings. Additionally, high output management practices promote environmentally sustainable approaches by reducing paper and ink consumption, contributing to a greener and more eco-friendly operational ecosystem.

Having a high-quality output management system in place is important for several reasons which include having efficiency and productivity, cost reduction, document integrity and consistency, security and compliance, analytics and reporting, integration and scalability, and having an enhanced customer experience.

A high-quality output management system is essential for organizations to improve efficiency, reduce costs, ensure document integrity, enhance security, deliver a superior customer experience, and achieve compliance with regulatory requirements. It plays a crucial role in optimizing document processes and facilitating effective communication within and outside the organization.

Furthermore, high output management ensures document integrity and consistency. By adhering to predefined templates, branding guidelines, and formatting standards, organizations can enhance their professional image and reduce the risk of errors or discrepancies in critical documents. This consistency not only reinforces the organization's brand identity but also inspires confidence and trust among stakeholders, including customers, partners, and employees.

In this book, you will learn the steps to getting high output management which is vital for organizations aiming to optimize their operations and achieve excellence in document-related processes. By implementing efficient output management practices, businesses can enhance productivity, reduce costs, ensure document integrity, and deliver an exceptional customer experience. Embracing high output management principles empowers organizations to navigate the ever-evolving business landscape with agility, efficiency, and a competitive edge.

CHAPTER 1

DEFINE YOUR PHILOSOPHY

Businesses need clear direction to thrive and grow. As a manager, crafting an inspiring vision and setting clear goals and strategies will allow your team to achieve high output. Defining your management philosophy lays the groundwork for everything that follows.

1. MANAGEMENT PHILOSOPHY

Start by writing down your core beliefs about how to manage people effectively. Consider questions like:

- How do I motivate and inspire people?

- How should I communicate and provide feedback?

- How do I build trust and accountability?

\-   How do I encourage teamwork and collaboration?

Your answers will shape how you hire, train, recognize, and lead your team.

What is Management Philosophy?

A management philosophy is a manager's set of core beliefs about how to most effectively lead people and organizations. It guides priorities, decisions and actions. A good management philosophy balances trust and accountability, autonomy and control, recognition and discipline. There are no universally right answers, but consistency is important to build trust.

A manager's philosophy is shaped by their personality, values, experience and organizational culture. It tends to evolve over time as the manager learns what works and what doesn't. Communicating a clear management philosophy to the team helps set expectations, build alignment and foster commitment. Employees want to understand the "why" behind how a manager leads.

Aligning goals, strategies and initiatives with a manager's philosophy ensures consistency in implementation. It helps create a unified culture where all efforts contribute to overall success.

Monitoring outcomes and gathering employee feedback allows a manager to refine their philosophy over time. Adjusting parts that don't seem to motivate or develop people effectively. An effective management philosophy balances competing priorities like short-term performance and long-term development, individual goals and team needs, innovation and risk control. There are rarely "right" answers on how to weigh these.

A manager's philosophy provides a moral compass and roadmap to lead people in a way that maximizes their potential and the organization's performance.

ANSWERING THE QUESTIONS ON MANAGEMENT PHILOSOPHY

First Question: How do I motivate and inspire people?

Different people are motivated in different ways. An effective manager tailors their motivation strategies based on understanding individual needs for autonomy, mastery, purpose, relationships and recognition. A combination of intrinsic and extrinsic motivators usually works best.

- Communicate a clear vision and goals. People want to know the purpose and impact of their work. An inspiring vision and meaningful goals can motivate people intrinsically.

- Show trust and give autonomy. People want to feel trusted to do their jobs well. Giving employees autonomy and input fosters motivation, engagement and ownership.
- Recognize and reward achievements. Positive feedback, rewards and incentives can motivate people, especially for more transactional tasks. But make sure recognition is genuine and tailored to individual needs.
- Develop talent and skills. People want to learn and grow in their jobs. Providing development opportunities, coaching and mentoring can motivate employees who crave mastery and growth.
- Create a supportive environment. A workplace with psychological safety, empathy and team spirit can motivate people who value belonging and relationships. Lead by example with positivity and compassion.

- Encourage innovation and improvement. Challenge employees with opportunities for creativity, new ideas and continuous improvement. People want to do meaningful work that makes an impact.
- Show appreciation and care. Simple gestures like thank you notes, birthday wishes and asking about personal lives can motivate people who value feeling valued as individuals, not just employees.
- Align work with purpose and values. People want to feel that their work contributes to a larger purpose and aligns with their ethics and values. Help connect the dots between individual roles and organizational mission.

Second Question: How should I communicate and provide feedback?

Feedback is information about how you're doing in a certain area that helps you improve. Clear, honest, frequent and two-way communication builds trust and motivates employees. Feedback in particular, when provided the right way, empowers people to grow and perform at a higher level.

- Be transparent and consistent. Share information openly and consistently with the team. Keeping people "in the loop" builds trust.

- Explain the why, not just the what. Provide the rationale and context behind decisions, goals and priorities. This helps people understand and buy in.

- Listen actively. Make an effort to truly understand employees' perspectives by listening without judgment and restating for clarity.

- Provide feedback frequently. Regular check-ins and coaching conversations, not just annual reviews, help people improve and grow in their roles.

- Focus feedback on behaviors, not people. Describe specific actions that were effective or need improvement, not general personality traits. This keeps it constructive.

- Separate performance from personal value. Remind people that you appreciate them as individuals regardless of any work-related feedback. This maintains self-esteem.

- Make feedback specific and actionable. Use concrete examples and suggest specific actions for employees to consider. Vague feedback is not helpful.

- Balance positive and negative feedback. People need to hear what they're doing well as much as where they can improve. A ratio of 3:1 positive to negative feedback often works best.

- Follow up on feedback. Check in after providing feedback to see how employees are interpreting it and whether they need any clarification or support for implementing suggestions.

- Seek feedback from employees. Ask for honest input on your own management style. Be willing to adjust based on what you learn in order to keep improving communication.

Third Question: How do I build trust and accountability?

Trust and accountability are two interconnected concepts that play crucial roles in personal relationships, organizational dynamics, and societal interactions. While they are distinct concepts, they are often intertwined and mutually reinforcing.

Trust can be defined as the belief or confidence that one person or entity has in another's reliability, integrity, and competence.

Accountability, on the other hand, refers to the responsibility and answerability of individuals or organizations for their actions, decisions, and results. It involves taking ownership of one's responsibilities, acknowledging mistakes, and being answerable to oneself and others.

- Be transparent. Share information openly with your team and explain your decisions and priorities. Lack of transparency breeds mistrust.

- Follow through. Do what you say you will do. If you make a commitment or promise, ensure you follow through. Consistency builds trust over time.

- Admit mistakes. When you make an error, own up to it and apologize genuinely. This shows humility and builds trust for next time.

- Give autonomy. Allow employees to make decisions within certain guidelines.

Micromanaging signals a lack of trust and breeds resentment.

- Provide support. When giving autonomy, provide the resources and coaching people need to succeed. This builds confidence in their abilities.

- Set clear expectations. Ensure team members understand what is required of them and how their work contributes to goals. Remove ambiguity.

- Establish accountability. Have frank discussions about roles and responsibilities. Call people out in a constructive manner when expectations are not met.

- Provide feedback. Regular coaching and performance check-ins keep people aware of where they stand and what they need to improve. This enables accountability.

- Recognize good work. When team members meet or exceed expectations, acknowledge and reward their performance publicly. This reinforces accountability.

- Address poor performance directly. If an individual is not meeting expectations, set clear performance improvement plans with milestones. Follow up regularly. Letting poor performance go unaddressed breeds mistrust.

Fourth Question: How do I encourage teamwork and collaboration?

This last question is also important as the others. The most collaborative teams have manager who break down barriers, create connections, model teamwork and foster an environment where members feel safe contributing their best work through cooperation and coordination with others. Below are some points on how to make this effective in your organisation.

- Foster communication - Encourage people to share information, ask questions and help each other. Open layouts and frequent informal interactions help.

- Reward group achievements - When setting goals and incentives, consider team or department-level metrics in addition to individual goals.

- Emphasize interdependence - Explain to people how their roles depend on and support others. Help them see the "bigger picture."

- Encourage sharing - Promote a culture where people share knowledge, resources, contacts and best practices freely with colleagues.

- Facilitate community - Create spaces and opportunities for people to connect and interact, like communal areas, fun activities and team outings.

-       Model collaboration - Lead by example by openly collaborating with and soliciting input from your own team and other departments.

-       Seek diverse input - When making decisions, solicit perspectives from a wide range of people, not just the most senior or vocal.

-       Lastly, create team-oriented incentives - Instead of just individual bonuses, provide group rewards when teams hit collective goals.

2. Set Goals and Strategies

With your management philosophy in mind, determine the 1-3 year goals for your team and department. These should be specific, measurable targets related to productivity, quality, customer satisfaction, and profitability.

1-3 year goals are long enough that you'll have time to implement and refine strategies based on progress, but short enough to feel urgent. Make sure you also establish interim milestones to monitor progress and make adjustments along the way.

Some examples of 1-3 year goals for defining your management philosophy could be:

• Increase employee engagement scores by 15% within 2 years. This shows you are effectively motivating and developing your team.

• Reduce employee turnover by 20% within 3 years. This indicates you are building trust and an environment where people want to stay.

• Improve team performance ratings by managers and customers by 10% within 2 years. This demonstrates your strategies for focusing the team are working.

• Increase the percentage of team members with clear development plans by 50% within 1 year. This shows you are effectively aligning goals and providing growth opportunities.

• Double the number of team-level initiatives within 3 years. This indicates you are successfully fostering teamwork, collaboration and innovation.

• Increase the percentage of employees who "strongly agree" they understand how their work contributes to goals by 30% within 2 years. This shows you are effectively explaining the "why" behind the work.

The key is to translate your high-level management philosophies into concrete, measurable goals that will indicate whether or not your approaches to motivation, communication, trust-building, development and collaboration are effective. The goals will likely vary by industry and role, but should focus on outcomes that matter most to the team and organization.

In determining the 1-3 year goals for your team, you don't only set your goals, you also build strategies to achieve them. Focus on a few high-leverage strategies that will make the biggest impact. Common strategies involve: improving processes, developing talent, innovating products, and acquiring resources.

The goals you set should ultimately provide a framework for evaluating whether or not defining your management philosophy at the outset is truly helping you achieve high output from your team.

3. Align the Team

When defining your management philosophy, there is the need to communicate your management philosophy, goals, and strategies clearly to your team. Explain why they matter and how everyone's role contributes. Get input, buy-in, and commitment from your people. Make sure goals are challenging but realistic.

The following will help you to achieve these:

1. Communicate your philosophy clearly - Explain in simple and concrete terms how you plan to motivate, develop and lead the team. Give examples of what this means in practice.

2. Explain why it matters - Provide the context for why you have chosen this particular philosophy. Tie it back to organizational goals and objectives to demonstrate relevance.

3. Get early input - Consult with team members before finalizing your philosophy to understand their perspectives and needs. Incorporate feasible suggestions.

4. Discuss goals and strategies - Walk the team through the goals you have set and the strategies you will use to achieve them. Explain how the management philosophy supports these plans.

5. Get buy-in on goals - Ask for team members' input on whether goals are realistic, relevant and motivating. Make revisions as needed to maximize commitment.

6. Align people's objectives - Ensure individual team member objectives are consistent with and contribute to overall team and department goals. This creates line of sight.

7. Highlight interdependence - Explain to people how their roles support and depend on others. Help everyone see how individual efforts link to collective success.

8. Reiterate frequently - Return to your management philosophy and goals regularly in

meetings, updates and conversations to keep them top of mind. Repetition builds clarity and alignment.

9. Check for understanding - Ask team members to explain in their own words what the philosophy means and how it relates to goals. Clarify any misconceptions.

10. Make adjustments - If you find that parts of your philosophy or goals are not resonating with people or driving the intended behaviors, be willing to adjust course. Listen to feedback and adapt to maintain buy-in and commitment.

A clear and consistent communication of your management philosophy and how it connects to team objectives is key to gaining alignment. But allow for input, clarify misunderstandings, and refine strategies as needed based on employee feedback and reactions. Alignment is an ongoing process that requires constant nurturing.

Review and Refine

In addition to the three keys previously mentioned, you may wish to revisit your management philosophy regularly. As you gain experience, you'll learn what works and what doesn't. Adjust your approach based on feedback, results, and changing business needs. Similarly, review your goals and strategies annually to ensure they're still relevant and effective at driving high output.

CHAPTER 2

FOCUS ON THE IMPORTANT, NOT JUST THE URGENT

In a world of constant interruptions, emails, notifications and demands on our attention, it can be easy for managers to get pulled into tasks that are simply urgent, not truly important. But focusing your time and energy on what really drives results is key to achieving high output.

Urgent tasks tend to be reactive, loud and impose immediate demands on our attention. Important tasks, though they rarely shout for our focus at the moment, contribute significantly to our long-term goals and priorities. As managers, we must train ourselves to distinguish between the two and then strictly guard our time for important work.

This chapter will provide strategies for focusing your efforts on what truly matters most. We'll look at how to classify and prioritize tasks, manage interruptions, streamline routine work and track how you actually spend your time. Applied consistently, these techniques can dramatically increase your productivity, impact and overall sense of progress towards your goals.

The first step is changing your mindset. You must decide that important tasks which drive results deserve more of your energy than urgent ones which simply make noise. Focus is a choice - choose wisely. With discipline and the right systems in place, you can learn to focus your time and attention on what really generates high output for your team and organization over the long run.

The strategies in this chapter, when implemented consistently, can liberate your time and mental bandwidth to make real strides towards your most meaningful objectives. So let's get started on focusing your efforts where they'll make the biggest difference.

1. Classify tasks as important vs. urgent

Many day-to-day tasks are urgent but not important. Focus your time on important priorities that drive long-term goals, not just what's loud and immediate. Analyze each task based on two dimensions:

• Urgency - How much immediate demand or pressure is placed on doing this task now? Tasks that impose near-term deadlines or consequences are more urgent.

• Importance - How much will doing this task contribute to your strategic objectives and priorities? Tasks that support key goals and initiatives are more important.

Use a table like this:

Importance	
High	**Low**

- Important & urgent tasks are priorities you must attend to immediately. Strike a balance between quality and speed for maximum impact.

- Urgent but not important tasks can often be delegated or streamlined. Avoid spending too much time on reactive, low-value work.

- Important but not urgent tasks deserve preserved time and focus. Block out periods on your calendar for proactively making progress on these strategic priorities.

- Unimportant & not urgent tasks should be automated, minimized or eliminated entirely. Don't waste time on work that doesn't drive key objectives.

- With practice, you'll get better at classifying tasks quickly based on the two criteria above. Then allocate your time accordingly:

- Over time, shift more of your efforts towards the important/strategic quadrant. And when a task is both urgent and important, ensure you make real progress - not just keep up - to reduce future urgency.

- Constantly evaluate how you're spending your hours each week. Are you focusing enough time on truly important work that drives high output? If not, adjust how you classify and prioritize your tasks going forward.

2. Create a "Focus Time"

Block out time on your calendar to work on important projects without interruption. Turn off notifications and close emails during this time. Block out recurring time on your calendar dedicated solely to focusing on your most strategic priorities. For example:

- 2 hours every morning before emails and meetings
- 1 - 2 full days per week with no external commitments
- 1/2 day every other Friday

During this time:

- Turn off email and instant messaging notifications
- Mute your phone and close your office door
- Use an app to disable distracting websites and apps
- Make a "do not disturb" sign for your office door

Only allow interruptions for true emergencies. Otherwise, preserve this time for accomplishing important tasks like:

- Writing strategic plans
- Developing new initiatives
- Creating new materials or content

- Analyzing data and information
- Researching and exploring new ideas
- Reviewing and improving key processes

By guarding blocks of time where you're free from distractions, you'll develop a sense of flow that allows you to delve deep into important work and make real progress.

Over time, move longer and more important projects into your "Focus Time." For example:

- Week 1: Write a presentation

- Week 2: Plan a new initiative

- Week 3: Create a training program

- Week 4: Review department processes

But stick to your designated times. Resist the urge to check emails or take calls, even if you're "between tasks." This undermines the whole system.

To colleagues:

- Explain your "Focus Time" strategy
- Set clear guidelines for how/when to interrupt you
- Provide updates after each block so they know what you accomplished

Establishing recurring focus times - and sticking to them - can train your brain to enter a higher gear for accomplishing important work that drives real results. Schedule your next "Focus Time" now!

3. Delegate urgent tasks

Give routine or reactive tasks to team members so you can concentrate on strategic work that only you can do.

(a) Identify tasks you currently spend a lot of time on that are more urgent than important. These could include:

- Responding to many emails

- Handling routine requests

- Troubleshooting minor issues

- Updating and maintaining records

(b) For each task, consider who on your team is best suited to take it over. Ideally someone:

- With appropriate skills and experience

- Who has capacity to take on more work

- Who would benefit from the responsibility

(c) Set up a meeting to discuss delegating the task. Explain:

- Why you want to delegate (to focus on more strategic work)

- What the task entails in specifics

- How often/much time it will require

- Any resources or support they'll need

(d) Agree on a trial period to test run the new arrangement. Ensure you:

- Provide training and guidelines up front

- Address any questions or concerns

- Check in periodically for feedback

(e) Once delegation is working smoothly, scale back your involvement gradually. Resist the urge to "help out" unless truly needed.

(f) Over time, delegate more routine tasks to the same individuals. You'll train them to effectively take over pieces of your own role, freeing up your bandwidth even further.

(g) Consider delegating urgent tasks to multiple team members and rotate them occasionally. This shares the work and builds versatility.

(h) Stay focused! Resist checking in too often on delegated tasks. Trust your team members and stick to working on strategies that only you can implement.

By delegating urgent tasks that clamor for your attention each day, you can reclaim time to focus on identifying and delivering on important initiatives that drive high output for the organization. Your team members will also benefit from the increased responsibility, autonomy and potential for growth that comes from taking over parts of your former role. Delegation is truly a win-win when approached intentionally and successfully implemented.

4. Say "no" to urgent requests

Learn to decline tasks that take you away from important work, even if they come from senior leadership. Politely explain your priorities.

As a manager, your limited time is one of your most valuable resources. You must choose carefully how you allocate your hours each day in order to maximize your impact. Many requests that come your way may be urgent, demanding an immediate response. But if they do not directly advance your most important goals and strategies, fulfilling those requests is unlikely to generate the greatest value for the organization.

So you must develop the discipline to politely but firmly turn down urgent tasks that would pull you away from the important work only you can do - the work that will truly drive high output for your team and department over the long term. Simply being "busy" does not correlate with being effective or productive. You achieve outcomes not by how active you are, but by where you choose to focus your efforts.

Saying "no" to distracting requests requires preparation, consistency and an emphasis on results over activity or effort. But done right, it allows you to preserve your limited hours for initiatives that will make the biggest impact.

That's the fundamental tradeoff successful managers must make - trading the perception of being "busy" for the reality of being purposeful in how they spend their time. By focusing on important work and guarding your time carefully, you can achieve significantly better outcomes with far less effort and stress.

So learn to say "no" politely yet firmly and confidently to urgent requests. Reallocating even a few hours a week from reactive tasks to proactive strategies can dramatically increase your productivity and contribution as a manager.

Your time is one of your greatest assets. Choose how you use it wisely in service of your most meaningful objectives. That's the essence of high output discipline.

5. Automate and streamline routine tasks

As a manager, many of the tasks you spend time on each day are repetitive, low-value activities that do not directly contribute to important goals or strategies. Use tools and checklists to minimize time spent on low-value repetitive work so you can shift focus to what truly matters.

Whether it's responding to many emails, reviewing reports, updating records or troubleshooting minor issues, these routine "busy work" tasks consume a significant amount of mental energy and time that could be better spent on more strategic initiatives.

However, many routine tasks can be partially or fully automated using tools and systems. This allows you to minimize or even eliminate the time spent on them, freeing up your bandwidth for higher value work.

Common automation approaches include:

- Email filters and templates
- Checklists and standard operating procedures
- Software to track data, record requests and process documents
- Decision trees and algorithms for common issues
- APIs and workflows to integrate different systems

Even tasks that cannot be fully automated can often be streamlined through standardization, delegation and redesigning processes to minimize non-value added steps.

By taking a critical eye to all the routine work you do each day - from answering emails to filling out forms - and then automating or streamlining as much of it as possible, you can potentially free up several hours each week for focusing on strategically important objectives instead.

The key is shifting your mindset from seeing routine tasks as "part of the job" to opportunities for minimizing effort through technology and process improvements. With enough discipline and creativity, you may even discover there are certain tasks your role no longer needs to do at all.

Automating and streamlining the "busy work" is an often overlooked yet highly effective strategy for managers seeking to maximize their impact and achieve truly high output.

So take inventory of all the repetitive tasks currently demanding your time and energy. Then explore how technology, systems and process redesign could minimize the time and effort you invest in them - freeing you up for the meaningful work only you can do.

6. Avoid perfectionism

Important work doesn't need to be perfect, just good enough to make progress. Reduce rework time spent aiming for 100% vs. 80%.

As managers, we often fall into the trap of pursuing perfect results before taking action or making progress on important initiatives. This perfectionistic tendency can significantly reduce our productivity and output.

When working on strategic priorities, a good enough solution that makes forward progress is almost always better than a perfect one that never materializes. Yet we allow ourselves to get bogged down in unnecessary details, redundantly revising work before sharing it, and over-analyzing decisions rather than just making them.

The costs of perfectionism include:

- Wasting huge amounts of time. Chasing "perfect" often triples or quadruples the hours needed to complete a task.

- Missing deadlines and opportunities. When trying to do everything flawlessly, you rarely end up doing anything at all.

- Discouraging creativity and risk-taking. The fear of making mistakes paradoxically inhibits coming up with your best ideas.

For important work to drive high output, it simply needs to be thorough enough by covering the key bases and answering the most essential questions. It should be clear enough to effectively communicate the core ideas in an organized manner. Lastly, it should be actionable enough to provide concrete next steps and recommendations.

"Perfect" is often the enemy of "good enough." And "good enough" leads to real progress, valuable learning and eventual improvement - whereas "perfect" often leads nowhere.

So when working on important initiatives, set a "good enough" standard up front. Define what would constitute a solid first pass worth sharing, testing or implementing. Stick to that bar. Resist the urge to keep revising beyond the "good enough" threshold just to eliminate minor flaws. Also learn from feedback. Refine your work based on real-world input, not theoretical possibilities. Adjust and improve incrementally. "Perfect" often exists only in the abstract. In practice, work evolves through a series of "good enough" iterations.

Remember, your most meaningful contributions as a manager often come from simply getting work started and putting plans into action. Further refinements will come along the way. So avoid perfectionism by setting "good enough" standards, sticking to them and learning by doing instead of endless hypothesizing. Focus on making progress, not achieving flawless results up front. That's the path to true high output.

7. Track your focus

Keep a log of how you actually spend your time. This will reveal where you're wasting effort on the urgent at the expense of the important.

Without tracking how you spend your time, it's easy to mistakenly give too much attention to urgent tasks. By keeping a log of your time usage, you gain insight into where your efforts are best applied and where they may be wasted. This allows you to make adjustments to optimize your focus and productivity:

- Set clearer priorities

- Delegate more tasks

- Guard your time carefully

- Improve your ability to say "no"

- Increase focus time for strategic work

Your ability to concentrate on important initiatives is a skill that improves through awareness and discipline. So start tracking how you spend your hours. You'll likely be surprised by how much "busy work" fills your weeks.

The awareness that time tracking provides will motivate you to make small adjustments that significantly increase your productivity over time. Focus follows awareness. So gain awareness of where your focus currently lands. Then redirect it towards what truly drives high output.

Tracking your time for even a few weeks - without changing anything else initially - can be a game changer. You'll soon find more minutes devoted to important work that makes the biggest difference.

In short, time tracking gives you visibility into how your attention is currently allocated. This insight allows you to deliberately refocus your efforts where they'll achieve the greatest results - the essence of high output discipline.

So start documenting how you use your minutes today. The first step to optimizing your focus is simply becoming aware of where it currently lands.

CHAPTER 3

BUILD A HIGH PERFORMING TEAM

One of a manager's main responsibilities is assembling and leading a team that delivers outstanding results. But creating a truly high performing team requires more than just hiring competent individuals - it demands a holistic approach.

This chapter will discuss strategies for building a team culture focused on excellence, accountability and collaboration.

• **Selecting the right people**

Hiring team members based on both technical skills and cultural fit. Looking for traits like initiative, resilience and adaptability.

- Clearly define the role. Identify key responsibilities, performance indicators and skills required. This forms the basis for assessing candidates.

- Look beyond resumes. Focus interviews on assessing cultural fit, motivations, strengths and potential based on behavioral and situational questions.

- Hire for aptitudes, not just skills. Look for traits like initiative, perseverance, collaboration and adaptability that predict future performance and growth.

- Cast a wide net. Source candidates from a diverse range of backgrounds and environments to find hidden gems. Don't rely solely on referrals.

- Make contingent offers. Consider "trying out" potential team members before committing permanently. This reduces risk and uncertainty.

- **Onboarding effectively**

Welcoming new hires in a way that quickly gets them up to speed and socially integrated into the team. Setting expectations and providing support.

- Assign a "buddy." Pair new hires with an existing team member to show them the ropes and make introductions.

- Create a checklist. Ensure all logins, equipment and resources are in place from day one.

- Share key info. Provide context on team/department goals, vital processes/systems and performance expectations.

- Set up meetings. Schedule 1:1s with manager and team members for the first few weeks.

- Provide guidance. Give examples, templates and coaching to accelerate productivity and confidence.

- **Developing talent**

Design individual development plans for each team member. Provide coaching, feedback, training and stretch opportunities for growth. By treating development as an ongoing process - not just a once-a-year review - and creating opportunities for people to strengthen and expand their skills, you can motivate and retain your strongest team members while building a culture of continuous learning.

- Assess strengths and needs. Gather 360 feedback to identify where team members excel and could improve.

- Create development plans. Outline concrete skills, experiences and support needed for growth.

- Coach consistently. Provide real-time feedback and guidance, not just annual reviews.

- Offer stretch assignments. Give opportunities to develop new skills by trying things just outside your comfort zone.

- Provide training. Recommend courses, seminars, conferences and workshops to build strengths.

- Rotate roles. Consider rotating team members through different tasks and responsibilities periodically.

- Mentor proactively. Introduce high potentials to other senior leaders for visibility and sponsorship.

• Aligning individual goals - Ensuring everyone's objectives contribute to and support the team's collective goals. Creating line of sight to shared success.

• Building trust - Establishing psychological safety, open communication and a no-blame culture. Encouraging risk-taking and knowledge sharing.

• Fostering accountability - Setting clear expectations and performance standards. Holding people responsible for results in a reasonable, consistent manner.

• Encouraging collaboration - Breaking down silos. Recognizing and rewarding team achievements over individual ones. Modeling team-first behavior yourself.

By implementing these strategies in an integrated way, you can transform a group of talented individuals into a cohesive unit that achieves results greater than the sum of its parts. Building - and constantly renewing - a high performing team should be the keystone of any manager's philosophy.

Begin to put these principles into practice. Your role as a leader will determine, to a large extent, how effectively your team works together to deliver outstanding outcomes. With the right focus and strategies, you can create a culture of excellence that leads to true competitive advantage for your organization.

CHAPTER 4

RECRUIT TOP TALENT

Recruiting the right people is the foundation for building a high performing team. The talent you bring in serves as both a complement and supplement to your current team members. Top outside hires can add new skills, diverse perspectives and fresh energy that elevates overall performance.

However, successfully attracting and selecting top candidates requires an intentional and multifaceted approach. You must go beyond simply posting a job listing and sifting through resumes to find the true gems.

This section will discuss strategies for sourcing, evaluating and attracting top outside talent that can help take your team to the next level. We'll cover casting a wide recruiting net, using interview questions that reveal actual fit and potential, testing candidates' skills in realistic ways, making compelling offers focused on growth and impact, and leveraging referrals from happy current employees.

The goal is to identify individuals who not only demonstrate technical competency for the role, but also exhibit the aptitudes, drive and cultural fit that predict high performance and likelihood of success within your team environment. And for roles that require specialized expertise, you may need to be willing to compensate top talent competitively.

By thoroughly evaluating the "whole candidate" and what truly motivates them through a rigorous yet holistic selection process, you give yourself the best chance of recruiting new hires who can both perform exceptionally themselves and help lift up those around them. And that's what builds a sustainably high performing team over time.

So let's get started on implementing strategies that will allow you to attract top outside talent capable of taking your team to the next level. The right mix of new skills, perspectives and energy - complementing your current team members' strengths - can be just what's needed to catapult performance to new heights.

Why do You Need to Recruit Top Talent?

Top talent can enhance team performance in measurable ways through the skills and expertise they contribute, the standards they set, the innovative perspectives they offer, the future leaders they represent, and the motivation they provide for existing staff members. They serve as force multipliers that help you achieve more with the resources you have.

So recruiting top talent should be a high priority in building a sustainably high performing team. The right new hires can make significant positive impacts that ripple throughout your whole group.

There are a few key reasons why recruiting top talent is essential for building a high performing team:

1. Add new skills and expertise: Top talent brings in specialized knowledge, experiences and strengths that likely don't already exist within your team. This expands the collective capabilities of the group.

2. Increase overall performance: High performers tend to raise the bar for others and set a standard of excellence that lifts up the entire team. Their strong work ethic and drive can be contagious.

3. Challenge status quo thinking: New recruits with diverse backgrounds and perspectives often question assumptions and propose creative solutions that advance the team's work in meaningful ways.

4. Fill future leadership roles: Top talent often consists of high potentials that can be groomed for future management and leadership positions within the organization. They represent the "bench strength" for the future.

5. Reduce workload for current staff: Recruiting top performers can take some pressure off your existing team members by distributing tasks and responsibilities across a wider pool of talented individuals.

6. Improve employee retention: Giving existing team members opportunities to work alongside top talent can motivate and challenge them, reducing their likelihood of seeking opportunities elsewhere.

7. Set an example for hiring: Bringing in exceptional new hires who demonstrate the potential and fit you're looking for provides a model or exemplar for future recruiting and interviewing.

How to Recruit Top Talent

By casting a wide net, thoroughly evaluating candidates' technical and "soft" skills, testing applicants realistically, and making a compelling offer focused on growth, impact and fit, you can recruit top outside talent to complement and enhance your current high performing team. The right hires will not only perform at a high level themselves but also help lift up those around them.

• Clearly define the role: Before you start looking for candidates, take time to define the responsibilities, skills and experience required for the position. This will help you evaluate applicants effectively.

• Cast a wide net: Source candidates from a variety of places, not just the "usual suspects." Think beyond job boards and consider universities, professional associations, niche forums and referral programs.

• Hire for both skills and potential: Look for evidence that candidates not only have the core technical skills for the role but also the attitude, curiosity and drive to grow into even greater responsibilities.

• Ask behavioral interview questions: Focus on examples from candidates' past experiences that demonstrate key traits you want in the role, like initiative, teamwork, resilience and adaptability. Avoid hypothetical questions.

• Test technical skills through real tasks: Give candidates sample projects, problems or case studies related to the position for them to solve. This provides a more realistic assessment of their abilities.

• Consider "tryout" periods: If possible, hire new team members on a probationary basis initially to evaluate their actual performance before committing permanently. This reduces risk.

• Negotiate salaries transparently: Discuss candidates' salary expectations and your budget range upfront. Be willing to compensate top talent competitively.

• Make a compelling offer: In addition to compensation, highlight development opportunities, level of responsibility, impact of the role, and cultural fit with your team to attract the best candidates.

• Seek referrals from current employees: Your happy team members are your best recruiters. Compensate them for successful referrals who join your team.

Benefits of Recruiting Top Talent

The following are potential positive effects when top talent is successfully recruited into an existing team:

- Higher overall performance - Top performers tend to raise the bar and set a standard of excellence that influences others to lift their game. Performance across the team can increase.

- Increased innovation - New recruits with diverse skills and perspectives often challenge the status quo and propose creative solutions that advance the team's work in meaningful ways.

- Enhanced capabilities - Top talent brings in specialized knowledge, experiences and strengths that likely don't already exist within the team. This expands the collective skill set and problem solving abilities.

• Improved staff retention - Giving existing team members opportunities to work alongside top performers can motivate and challenge them, reducing their likelihood of seeking opportunities elsewhere.

• Examples of excellence - Having exemplary new hires demonstrates to the rest of the team what "top talent" looks like and provides a model for future recruiting and interviewing.

• Enhanced reputation - Attracting and retaining top outside talent enhances the perceived reputation and desirability of the team as an organization to work for. This advantage compounds over time.

• Future leadership pipeline - Top talent often consists of high potentials who can be mentored and developed into future management and leadership positions within the organization. They represent future bench strength.

• Improved workload distribution - Recruiting top performers takes some pressure off existing staff by distributing tasks and responsibilities across a wider pool of talented individuals. Burnout risks diminish.

• Motivation through challenge - Working alongside top talent can motivate and challenge existing team members, improving their skills and performance through healthy competition and knowledge sharing.

In summary, successfully recruiting top outside talent into an existing team can have many positive ripple effects: from directly enhancing performance, capabilities and workload distribution to serving as examples, boosting reputation and developing future leaders. The effects reinforce each other in a virtuous cycle that sustains high performance over time.

CHAPTER 5

DEVELOP YOUR PEOPLE

Your team members are one of your greatest assets as a manager. By investing in their growth and unleashing their potential, you unlock tremendous value for your organization.

Developing your people should be a continuous process that nurtures talent, expands capabilities and motivates high performance over the long run. But it requires a holistic and proactive approach beyond simply assigning tasks and reviewing annual performance.

This part of the chapter will discuss strategic and integrated ways you can develop the individuals on your team into high performers who drive meaningful business results. We'll cover:

- Hiring for potential, not just current skills

- Providing an effective onboarding experience

- Aligning individual development goals with team and organizational objectives

- Offering opportunities for on-the-job learning, coaching and stretch assignments

- Recognizing and celebrating progress toward development goals

By focusing on nurturing potential over just managing current performance, you can transform the people on your team into top talent who increase the capabilities and future adaptability of your whole organization.

So let's discuss implementing a systematic approach to developing your team members into high performers - and ultimately into future leaders. The time you invest in elevating the skills, experiences and mindsets of the individuals in your charge will yield tremendous returns for you and your organization in both the short and long term.

With the right strategies and support, you can unlock the full potential within your team - potential that will drive your shared success for years to come. The journey starts by treating development as an integral part of your job, and the returns will come back to you many times over.

1. Hiring for potential, not just current skills

Focus on a candidate's ability and willingness to learn, adapt and grow, rather than just their current roster of skills and experience. Individuals with high potential exhibit traits like:

• Learnability and adaptability - The ability and desire to take on new skills and information quickly, and adapt to changing needs and environments.

• A growth mindset - The belief that skills and abilities can be developed with effort, rather than being fixed traits. This motivates employees to continuously improve.

• Motivation beyond salary - High performers seek challenging work, impact, opportunities for advancement and professional growth, not just compensation.

• Ability to learn from failures - Superior employees can articulate valuable lessons learned from past challenges and mistakes, rather than just success stories.

• Eagerness to be stretched - They welcome opportunities that push their limits and expand their skillset, comfort zone and responsibilities.

By prioritizing these potential traits over just a candidate's current qualifications and resume, you give yourself the best chance of hiring individuals who will develop into your highest performers and future leaders over time.

The key is focusing on a candidate's potential - their ability and willingness to learn, adapt and grow into the roles you need filled. Top performers often don't have all the required skills initially, but do possess the aptitude, motivation and mindset to develop them quickly.

2. Providing an effective onboarding experience

In short, providing an effective onboarding experience for new hires means welcoming team members in a structured yet supportive way that quickly gains them traction and sets them up for long-term success.

The goal of onboarding is to help new employees:

* Reach full productivity as quickly as possible

- Understand organizational goals, policies and expectations

- Connect with the people and resources they need to do their job

- Adjust and integrate into the company culture

- Feel welcomed, supported and motivated in their new role

This is achieved through:

- Assigning mentors or buddies to guide them

- Creating a structured onboarding plan with goals and milestones

- Providing the resources, tools and information they need upfront

- Clearly communicating performance expectations

- Fostering connections with key internal and external colleagues

- Offering ongoing support and answering questions

- Sharing cultural norms, habits and behaviors that exemplify company values

The benefits of an effective onboarding process are:

- Higher retention of new hires

- Faster time to productivity and value creation

- Greater job satisfaction and motivation

- Improved continuity and knowledge transfer

- Faster integration into the team and organization

So in essence, onboarding is not just about the first day, it's about the first days, weeks and months - ensuring new team members quickly gain their footing and align with your organization's goals, needs and culture in a way that sets the stage for high performance and long-term contribution.

3.   Aligning individual development goals with team and organizational objectives

Individual development goals should support organizational objectives to have maximum impact.

Why align goals?

Individual growth directly enables organizational success when:

• Development addresses skills gaps limiting key priorities

• Individuals expand abilities in areas needed most by the team and company

• New skills allow team/organization to achieve important goals

Benefits of aligned goals:

- Improved individual performance

- Achievable team/organizational goals

- Increased business results

Everyone benefits when individual development:

- Builds capabilities required for organizational success

- Eliminates knowledge gaps holding back performance at all levels

How to align goals:

Start with organizational needs and priorities, then:

- Determine skills gaps preventing success

- Set individual development goals that build needed skills

- Ensure goals are specific, measurable and tied to incentives

The result is optimized growth that yields greatest impact by:

- Directly enabling higher performance

- Eliminating strategic knowledge gaps

Aligned development goals motivate individuals while ensuring their growth directly drives progress on key team and organizational objectives. Individual growth translates into business results.

4. Offering opportunities for on-the-job learning, coaching and stretch assignments

Much of employee development happens through day-to-day work and hands-on experiences, not just formal training. As a manager, you can facilitate this on-the-job learning by:

•   Providing coaching: Discuss projects in real time to guide team members, provide feedback and correct missteps early.

•   Assigning stretch projects: Give opportunities to work on tasks just outside their comfort zone that build new skills and capabilities.

•   Rotating roles and responsibilities: Periodically swap people into different functions so they gain diverse experiences and strengths.

•   Pairing with mentors: Connect team members with senior employees who can advise, guide and model best practices.

•   Sponsoring learning resources: Recommend and fund courses, workshops programs and certification relevant to their growth.

• Giving actionable feedback: Discuss what someone did well, how they can improve and specific recommendations to apply next time.

• Supporting through obstacles: Be available to answer questions and remove roadblocks so people can learn through overcoming challenges.

The key is balancing opportunities that:

• Build targeted skills and knowledge aligned with individual development goals

• Stretch people enough to significantly expand their abilities but with enough support initially

Combining on-the-job learning experiences with coaching, feedback and guidance can accelerate growth and maximize the benefit team members derive from their day-to-day work.

Look for natural opportunities within people's roles and projects to provide coaching, stretch assignments, mentorship, resources and feedback that develop capabilities exactly when and where they're needed most.

5. Recognizing and celebrating progress toward development goals

Highlighting milestones along team members' development journeys sustains motivation and ties their growth directly to incentives and advancement. As a manager, you can:

• Express appreciation: Thank people for efforts toward self-improvement, willingness to take on stretch assignments, and seeking out learning opportunities.

• Acknowledge milestones: Formally recognize when individuals achieve development goals, gain new certifications, or complete impactful training programs.

• Link to incentives: Tie achievement of development goals to raises, bonuses, promotions, preferred job assignments, or other tangible rewards.

• Provide visibility: Recommend high performers for leadership programs, spot bonuses, or mention in company communications to signal their development and progress.

• Highlight contributions: Discuss how individuals' newly acquired skills and strengths are directly contributing to team and organizational objectives.

• The key is to recognize and celebrate progress regularly and publicly to reinforce that:

• Development is important and valued within your team culture

• Growth leads directly to incentives, advancement and career opportunities

• Impactful contributions are recognized and rewarded

Regular recognition motivates individuals to continue investing in their own development, while tying achievement of development goals to tangible outcomes ensures their efforts remain focused and impactful.

So celebrate progress toward development goals publicly and frequently - and connect that progress directly to incentives and opportunities for growth. Make it clear that developing one's skills and strengths is how people advance their careers within your team and organization.

CHAPTER 6

EMBRACE CHANGE AND INNOVATION

Leading effective change and fostering a culture of innovation within your team is key to remaining relevant, productive and competitive over time. But navigating change successfully requires intentional strategies, an open mindset and involve your people every step of the way.

This section will discuss proactive ways you can embrace change and nurture innovation within your team. We'll cover:

• Seeing change as an opportunity for growth rather than a threat

• Assigning "change champions" within the team to pilot and promote new ideas

• Experimenting, evaluating and iteratively improving new approaches quickly

- Promoting a culture that rewards creativity, risk-taking and learning from failures

- Continuously seeking ways to improve processes and ways of working

The goal is to develop a team that can proactively drive change from within rather than simply reacting to changes others initiate. By adopting a flexible mindset, cultivating an innovative culture and involving your people throughout, you can lead your team through necessary transformations that enable you to achieve greater results over time.

So let's discuss implementing strategies that will allow you to embrace change and nurture innovation within your team. An openness to new ideas, a tolerance for risk and experimentation, and a willingness to learn from missteps will be key mindsets.

With the right approaches, structures and cultures in place, your team can leverage change and fresh perspectives as opportunities for growth that ultimately propel you forward. Leading effective transformation starts with the attitudes, habits and processes you instill within your own team - so let's dive into how you can nurture an innovative and adaptive team mindset from the inside out.

1.   Seeing change as an opportunity for growth rather than a threat

Change represents an opportunity for growth and progress. Resist clinging to the comfort of the status quo. While familiarity feels safe, staying the same ultimately leads to stagnation. Embrace inevitable change.

Focus on the potential benefits change creates. What opportunities does it unlock? What progress does it enable? How will outcomes or performance improve? Shift the narrative from disruption to one of positive transformation.

Communicate a compelling vision for the future state. Paint a picture of what success looks like after change is implemented. This inspires enthusiasm and motivates people through the transition.

Highlight the growth and learning opportunities change provides. Individuals' skills, knowledge and careers can benefit tremendously from navigating change successfully. Appeal to their self-interest.

Change loosens constraints, enabling fresh perspectives and innovative solutions to emerge. Focus on the new possibilities that becoming untethered from current ways of working makes possible.

Recognize negative emotions like fear and uncertainty are natural reactions to change.

Acknowledge people's feelings while appealing to a higher purpose or beneficial outcomes.

Model positive excitement and enthusiasm yourself as you lead through change. Your mindset and outlook influences others. Focus your own energy on thriving through rather than resisting change. Lead from the front.

View change as an opportunity for growth, progress, innovation and even reinvention. By cultivating a positive, possibility-focused mindset and communicating a compelling vision, you pave the way for your team to embrace transformation and emerge stronger. An opportunity mindset is infectious - spread it within your team to catalyze innovation and progress.

2.   Assigning "change champions" within the team to pilot and promote new ideas

Identifying change champions within your team is important for successfully navigating transformation. Change champions can:

• Pilot new ideas on a smaller scale initially. They act as test cases for how changes may impact performance, processes and morale. Their experiences provide insights to refine changes before widescale implementation.

• Gather feedback from teammates. Change champions can get input from others who are more skeptical about how potential changes might impact work. They bring this diverse input to inform improvements.

• Promote adoption of new approaches. By publicly supporting and demonstrating value in changes, champions influence others to adopt innovations more quickly. Their buy-in convinces fence-sitters.

• Receive visibility and recognition. Acknowledge champions openly for their risk-taking, leadership and pioneering new approaches. This signals that innovation is valued and incentivizes others to step into champion roles for future changes.

• Be paired with more skeptical employees. Partnering change champions with those resistant to transformation provides opportunities to directly address concerns, reduce uncertainty and gain important conversions.

So identify individuals within your team already open to new ideas and assign them change champion roles. Provide support but also visibility, recognition and rewards to motivate others to step into similar positions for the next change initiative. And partner champions with those most skeptical to directly promote buy-in and adoption. Change champions accelerate navigating transformation successfully within your team.

3. Experimenting, evaluating and iteratively improving new approaches quickly

Start small. Try new ideas and changes on a limited scale first with only a few willing volunteers. This allows testing impacts with minimal disruption if issues arise. Problems caught early are easier to fix.

• Define success metrics. Determine what key indicators will show if the change is achieving its intended outcomes and innovation goals. Gather both quantitative and qualitative data.

• Continuously monitor. As the change is implemented on a small scale, solicit frequent feedback and monitor relevant metrics. Look for problems, unintended consequences or areas for improvement. Make adjustments.

• Make iterative improvements. Based on learnings from initial implementation, quickly make refinements to processes, tools, trainings or other aspects of the change before scaling further. Iterate through multiple Plan-Do-Check-Act cycles.

• Scale gradually. Expand changes incrementally to allow for ongoing learning and refinement at each stage. Moving too fast can limit your ability to course correct as needed.

• Focus on progress, not perfection. Changes can always be optimized further. The goal is not a flawless first attempt, but gaining enough momentum to keep improving based on real-world experience implementing the change.

• Accept trade-offs and hiccups. All changes will have unintended consequences and obstacles. Expect issues as you test new ideas in practice. The key is learning from them to make subsequent iterations more impactful.

• Set timelines and criteria. Determine clear milestones and criteria for evaluating whether a new approach should proceed or be revised substantially based on your monitoring. Not all changes work.

• Frame iterations positively. View refinements and improvements as positive signs of progress and learning, not negatives that undermine buy-in. Reinforce that change is an ongoing process of experimentation, adjustment and progress.

Experimenting on a small scale, continuously monitoring key indicators, rapidly iterating based on learnings and slowly scaling changes enables you to maximize benefits while minimizing drawbacks. This optimize your chances of realizing the goals of transformation within your team.

4. Promoting a culture that rewards creativity, risk-taking and learning from failures

Innovation requires an environment where people feel comfortable thinking differently, experimenting with new approaches and learning from both successes and mistakes. Cultivating such a culture within your team unlocks creative potential and drives progress.

The key is establishing cultural norms that value:

• Creativity -generate many novel ideas, even impractical ones

• Risk-taking -test new approaches, even if uncertainties exist

• Learning from failures -view "failures" as data points, not dead ends

Promoting a culture that rewards creativity, risk-taking and learning from failures requires communicating innovation is a valued behavior, reframing "failures" as learning opportunities, giving teams permission to experiment, protecting resources for ideation, role modeling risk-taking yourself, establishing psychological safety, asking questions that stimulate novel ideas, and providing frequent, process-oriented feedback. The right cultural conditions unleash innovation potential within any team.

- Reward creative ideas and innovative solutions - even those that don't pan out - to encourage out-of-the-box thinking. Recognize efforts, not just outcomes.

- Offer visibility and career advancement for those who champion change, take intelligent risks and think differently. Signal this behavior is valued.

• Accept that some experiments and innovations will fail. Focus on what was learned, not the failure itself. View failures as data points, not dead ends.

• Reframe "failures" as "learnings" to reduce stigma and encourage more risk-taking. Focus on the knowledge gained to inform future efforts.

• Explicitly give team members permission to test new ideas, even if uncertainties exist. Communicate an expectation of experimentation.

• Protect time and resources for exploration, ideation and innovation. Carve out slots in meetings, allocate innovation budgets, justify "think time."

• Openly share stories of innovative successes - and constructive failures to inspire others. Normalize risk-taking and learning from failures/learnings.

•   Establish psychological safety where people feel comfortable speaking up with creative ideas, diverse opinions and experiments that may not pan out.

•   Ask open-ended questions that stimulate fresh perspectives and new ways of thinking. Inquire "what if?" and "why not?" rather than "why?"

•   Give frequent, specific feedback focused on processes over outcomes. Praise improvements in thinking, methodology and iterative refinement.

5.   Continuously seeking ways to improve processes and ways of working

At its core, continuously seeking ways to improve processes and ways of working means having a mindset of ongoing self-improvement, refinement and optimization within your team. Some key aspects include:

• Regularly soliciting feedback from team members on how work is done, what's working well and what could be better. Gather input through surveys, one-on-ones, and team meetings.

• Reviewing policies, norms, systems and workflows to identify where updates or streamlining could enable better results. Critically examine everything.

• Removing obstacles, barriers or constraints that inhibit productivity, motivation or innovation within processes. Identify and remove roadblocks.

• Implementing small but impactful changes based on feedback and input from the team. Even minor tweaks can have a big effect.

• Iteratively testing and refining new approaches based on how well they achieve intended outcomes. Continuously reevaluate effectiveness.

• Monitoring evolving needs, technologies or industry best practices to inform ways of working within your team. Stay abreast of changes.

• Recognizing and rewarding teams that identify opportunities for improvement and embrace change. Signal that constant optimization is valued.

The key is cultivating a culture where everyone seeks to identify ways to do things better, smarter or more efficiently and where implemented changes are then reexamined for further refinement. Continuous improvement should be an ongoing habit and mindset within your team.

So at its heart, continuously improving processes means proactively looking for ways to optimize, streamline and enhance how work gets done on an ongoing basis. The goal is to relentlessly drive out inefficiencies, obstacles and unnecessary complexities that stand in the way of achieving the best results.

Process improvement and optimization should be viewed as an ongoing pursuit within your team - not a single project with a clear start and end. Maintaining a lens of "how can we do this better?" will fuel incremental enhancements that compound over time.

CHAPTER 7

BALANCE STRESS AND DRIVE

Looking at today's fast-paced work environment, you will notice that a certain amount of stress is inevitable. But not all stress is created equal. The key is distinguishing between eustress that motivates and energizes vs distress that overwhelms and impairs.

For peak productivity and employee wellbeing, people need strategies to harness the benefits of positive stress while minimizing the negative impacts of excessive pressure. This requires:

• Identifying sources of eustress vs distress within work

• Developing personal coping mechanisms and mindset shifts

- Creating supportive structures, processes and role modeling at an organizational level

- Fostering a sustainable work rhythm that allows for recharge and recovery

- Spotting signs of unhealthy distress in others and providing support

- Shifting culture to recognize activities that promote sustainability and balance

This chapter will discuss:

- Understanding the differences between eustress and distress

- Identifying stressors within your work that fall on each end of the spectrum

- Applying techniques to mitigate negative distress and maximize the benefits of eustress

• Implementing systems, flexibility and role modeling that promote sustainable performance

• Establishing a healthy work rhythm that regularly incorporates breaks and recharge time

The aim is helping people harness the power of positive stress while avoiding the unsustainable overload of negative distress - maximizing productivity without burningout your team. Let's discuss strategies for integrating balance and sustainability alongside drive and motivation within your organization's culture.

1. Understanding the differences between eustress and distress

Eustress refers to positive stress that motivates, energizes and enhances performance. It comes from challenges that align with skills and interests.

Examples of eustress include:

- Taking on an interesting new project

- Pursuing opportunities for growth

- Working toward meaningful goals

Distress refers to negative stress that overwhelms, causes anxiety and impairs performance. It comes from demands that exceed abilities or span of control.

Examples of distress include:

- Unrealistic deadlines

- Unclear or conflicting expectations

- Constant interruptions and overload

The same stressor can be eustress for one person but distress for another, depending on skills, interests and resources.

Eustress tends to energize people and expand abilities temporarily. Distress depletes energy and shrinks abilities over time. Eustress has an identifiable source and time limit. Distress often feels diffuse and endless.

People cope differently with eustress vs distress. The former may motivate people to work harder while the latter often makes people want to avoid or escape the situation.

Learning to harness eustress and mitigate distress

- Identifying sources within your specific work

- Developing mindfulness to alter your stress response

- Creating structures that nurture productivity and sustainability

Understanding these differences - and identifying specific stressors within your own work that fall on each end of the spectrum is key to establishing strategies that minimize distress while optimizing eustress for maximum productivity and employee wellbeing.

2. Identifying stressors within your work that fall on each end of the spectrum

Make a list of tasks, projects and demands within your work. For each one, ask yourself:

- Does this challenge align with my skills/interests? (eustress)

- Does this overwhelm my abilities or capacity? (distress)

Look for patterns among stressors you identified as eustress vs distress. What common themes emerge?

Consider factors beyond the tasks themselves:

- Can I control or influence the demands? More control = potential eustress

- Do I have adequate resources and flexibility? Less flexibility/resources = likely distress

For sources of eustress, think of ways to increase the challenge while keeping it aligned with your skills. Consider how you can leverage this positive stress as motivation to perform at your best.

For sources of distress, brainstorm ways to reduce, reshape or eliminate the demand. Think of resources, flexibility or support that could alleviate the overwhelm

Also, pay attention to physiological and psychological responses:

-    Does your energy/motivation increase or decrease?

-    Do you feel in control or at the mercy of external demands?

Set limits on distressing tasks and negotiate for more resources/flexibility where possible.

Leverage sources of eustress to motivate you through tasks causing distress.

The key is developing awareness of which demands energize you vs overwhelm you - and then applying strategies to minimize overly distressing aspects of your work while taking advantage of opportunities for productive eustress.

3. Applying techniques to mitigate negative distress and maximize the benefits of eustress

There are several measures than can be taken to mitigate distress. Some of them are discussed below:

• Practice mindfulness techniques - Deep breathing, progressive muscle relaxation, meditation, etc. These can help calm anxiety and frustration.

• Reframe - Try looking at distressing stressors in a more positive light. Focus on opportunities for growth, learning, or impact rather than overwhelm.

• Set limits and boundaries - Say "no" more often, delegate or remove tasks causing unsustainable distress. Negotiate for more resources if possible.

• Break up large tasks into smaller chunks - This can make overwhelming demands feel more manageable. Tackle one piece at a time.

• Seek support - Talk to colleagues, managers, or mentors. Their perspectives, advice and assistance can help alleviate distress.

• Incorporate breaks - Step away from the source of distress periodically. Take a few minutes to recenter and recharge.

To maximize eustress:

• Savor the challenge - Focus on aspects you enjoy about the task. Relish the opportunities for growth and development it provides.

• Break goals into milestones - Having smaller targets along the way can maintain motivation and momentum.

• Limit distractions - Minimize or remove disruptions that could prevent you from fully engaging with the eustress-inducing task.

• Seek feedback - Get input from others to improve your approach, thinking and results. Their perspectives can help you take advantage of the learning opportunity.

• Reflect regularly- Take time to process how the experience is enhancing your skills, knowledge and abilities. This reinforces the benefits of the eustress.

• Reward yourself - Celebrate milestones and accomplishments along the way. This positive reinforcement motivates you to keep pushing yourself.

To maximize productivity, focus techniques on respectively reducing overwhelm from distressing stressors while enhancing engagement with eustress-inducing challenges. Mindfulness, reframing, breaking tasks down, and seeking support can help mitigate distress, while focusing on opportunities for growth, seeking feedback and self-reflection can help maximize eustress.

4. Implement systems, flexibility and role modeling that promote sustainable performance

Here are some ways to implement systems, flexibility and role modeling that promote sustainable performance:

- Set clear expectations - Provide specificity around workload, deadlines and responsibilities to reduce uncertainty and potential overwhelm.

- Offer adequate resources - Ensure people have the tools, technology, budget and staffing needed to complete tasks at a sustainable pace.

- Build in flexibility - Allow flexibility in work schedules, locations and number of hours to accommodate personal needs and recharge time.

- Incorporate breaks - Give people autonomy over when and how long to take breaks. Consider offering wellness rooms and mindfulness activities during the workday.

• Encourage time off - Promote employees to fully unplug and recharge by taking allotted vacation and leave time.

• Adjust workload - Modify assignments, projects or responsibilities for people showing signs of excessive distress.

• Communicate value of breaks - Explain how recharge time enables employees to do their best work, rather than detracting from productivity.

• Lead by example - Set boundaries around availability. Make time for rejuvenation part of your routine as a role model for your team.

- Spot signs early - Notice changes in behavior, mood or performance that indicate a person may be overwhelmed. Check in and offer flexibility.

- Provide support - Connect employees to resources such as counseling, wellness programs, employee assistance programs or coaches that can help.

Implementing systems like flexibility in schedules, clearly defined expectations and adequate resources, while also role modeling boundaries, time off and recharge, sets your organization up for sustainable performance over the long haul. Your team will be most productive when you empower people to avoid excessive distress by recharging between periods of eustress. So structure your policies, processes and leadership to incentivize productivity with balance and sustainability.

5. Establishing a healthy work rhythm that regularly incorporates breaks and recharge time

In today's 24/7 work environment, it's easy to become consumed by our tasks and obligations. But maintaining a sustainable pace requires intentionally building recharge time into our daily rhythms.

A healthy work rhythm alternates between periods of intense focus and intervals of relaxation or rejuvenation. This cycle guards against the negative impacts of prolonged stress while optimizing productivity in the time we do work.

To establish such a rhythm, identify ways to:

• Schedule breaks throughout your day. Set aside time for meals, stretching breaks, etc.

• Limit total work hours. Establish start/end times and stick to them

• Fully disconnect at night: Resist checking work emails after a certain hour

• Incorporate movement: Take walks and stretch breaks during high-intensity times

• Focus on one task at a time. Switch contexts fully when transitioning projects

• Lean on teammates when taking time off. Request coverage so you can fully recharge

Pay attention to your energy levels and adjust times/frequencies of breaks as needed. The goal is to experiment and customize a schedule that allows you to work intensely while preventing prolonged distress.

By intentionally structuring periods of work alongside recovery, you'll establish a sustainable cadence for maximum productivity and motivation over the long haul. A healthy work rhythm guards against burnout by periodically refueling your reserves.

So think carefully about how to build breaks, disconnect times and recharge periods into your daily routine. Experiment with different schedules and monitor their impact on your energy, focus and performance. Then refine and adjust and repeat. Over time, you'll establish a personalized rhythm that supports your most productive and balanced self.

CLOSING CHAPTER

HIGH OUTPUT STARTS WITH YOU

The overarching theme is shifting management focus from keeping busy and following processes to achieving meaningful outcomes that generate value for the organization. Output-oriented management maximizes productivity by clearly defining desired results, empowering teams and holding people accountable for achieving those objectives.

Focus on output, not activity. Manage for results, not just keeping busy. Set clear objectives and track progress against them.

Start with the end in mind. Be intentional about outcomes. Clarify goals, priorities and purpose before diving into action.

Demand output accountability. Hold people and teams responsible for achieving specific, measurable outcomes. Provide consequences for poor output and rewards for high output.

Give high-output people more responsibility. Empower and motivate your best performers by assigning them more meaningful work that utilizes their talents.

Match people to outputs. Put the right people in roles that align with their skills, interests and motivations. This optimizes outputs.

Clarify authority and responsibility. Define decision rights, resources and accountabilities for each role to avoid confusion and conflicts.

Use output-based measures. Monitor key performance indicators that reveal whether desired outputs are being achieved. Reduce dependence on activity-based metrics.

Shorten the chain of command. Eliminate unnecessary approvals and decision layers to accelerate outputs and reduce bureaucracy.

Increase autonomy to raise output. Provide more freedom, flexibility and discretion to teams and individuals to enable self-management focused on achieving outputs.

Engage employees in output-based problem solving. Involve people in identifying obstacles to outcomes and generating solutions to remove those barriers.

www.ingramcontent.com/pod-product-compliance
Lightning Source LLC
Chambersburg PA
CBHW062327290526
45794CB00005B/1935